POWERED ON

by Sarah Churman

INDIGORIVER
PUBLISHING

POWERED ÖN

The **SOUN**DS I choose to hear & the **NOISE** I don't

Sarah Churman

Editors: Adam Tillinghast, Matthew Jordan, Donna Melillo
Cover Design: Jason Kauffmann / Firelight Interactive / firelightinteractive.com
Page Design and Layout: Rick Soldin / book-comp.com
Cover Photograph: Kelli Ahern / Nine Photography / ninephotography.com
Additional Photography: Luis Peña, Misty Adams, Kelli Ahern, and Whitnae Churman
Back Cover Photograph: Rick Gilbert

Indigo River Publishing
3 West Garden Street Ste. 352
Pensacola, FL 32502
www.indigoriverpublishing.com

Ordering Information:
Quantity sales: Special discounts are available on quantity purchases by corporations, associations, and others. For details, contact the publisher at the address above.

Orders by U.S. trade bookstores and wholesalers: Please contact the publisher at the address above.

Printed in the United States of America

Library of Congress Control Number: 2012952414

ISBN 978-0-9856033-5-9

First Edition

With Indigo River Publishing, you can always expect great books, strong voices, and meaningful messages.
Most importantly, you'll always find ... words worth reading.

I want to dedicate this book to my 2 daughters: Olivia Li and Elise An. May you continue to grow into unique Godly individuals, always dance to the beat of your own drum, and continually find beauty in all things. I love you both more than you will ever know.

—Mom

"Spread love everywhere you go: first of all in your own house. Give love to your children, to your wife or husband, to a next door neighbor ... Let no one ever come to you without leaving better and happier. Be the living expression of God's kindness; kindness in your face, kindness in your eyes, kindness in your smile, kindness in your warm greeting."

—Mother Theresa

One

POP! I was eighteen months old the day my mom snuck up behind me with a brown paper bag and popped it, anxiously awaiting my reaction. When I gave none, her heart immediately sank.

Afterwards, she cried—and not just because of the confirmation that I had a hearing problem or the uncertainty about my future. My mom cried because of the times she had spanked my hand for getting into something I shouldn't have, or gotten frustrated when I seemed to have ignored her or my father. I remember her telling me one time, "We just thought you were going through the terrible twos a little early."

Nothing changed for me in the moment that my mom popped that bag, of course, but what it revealed would alter the way I would fit into the world around me for years to come …

Two

My earliest memory as a child was sitting under a little plastic blue elephant slide at daycare. I sat there and watched all the kids running around. As strange as it seems, I distinctly remember thinking to myself, "Why are their mouths moving?" I can't explain it, but I knew then that something was off.

It was after the defining moment of the "bag pop" that my parents started setting up doctors' appointments and taking me to audiologists for testing. This was in 1982, and science and technology were not what they are today. The doctors told my parents that my deafness was caused by certain medicines that were given to me at birth since my mother had developed an infection during labor and I was born with a fever. Many years later, I would discover that the cause of my deafness was something else entirely; but for the first twenty-one years of my life, I lived with that answer.

I was eventually fitted with hearing aids around the age of two; but even with the hearing aids, voices were muffled and distorted (think adults on *Charlie Brown*). Some sounds were there, but there was very little clarity or definition. Thunderstorms were nonexistent unless there was a loud crack just outside my house. You see, for many people like me, being deaf isn't necessarily about silence or complete lack of sound; it's about interpreting the few sounds that do come through.

Soon after I got my hearing aids, I started attending a deaf education school. There, I took speech classes, had speech therapy, and spent the day with a class full of other kids who wore hearing aids, cochlear implants, and other hearing devices. I was taught sign language, how to read lips, how to form words, how to pay attention to how people move their mouths, tongue placement, teeth placement, the rise and fall of a chest, and vibrations.

I have some fond memories of that school, the teacher, and the other students. My mother said she used to cry watching me get on the bus in the morning sometimes. She said I just climbed right on like a big girl and seemed to enjoy going to school. I do remember looking forward to it. We did a lot of fun activities like performing a play all in sign. I was Snow White and wore a "wig" of black hair made out of construction paper to cover my cottony, blonde hair. As you know, Snow White is kissed by the prince. That play is where I had my first kiss. The boy's name was Phillip, and he became my "boyfriend." One time, my sweet prince stuck an eraser so far up his nose that he had to go to the hospital to get it removed. He also broke my lunchbox when I let him use it as a stool to reach the spout on the water fountain. My mom was so mad, but she just didn't understand how important it was for me to help my boyfriend get a drink. Eventually, I was old enough for public school and was deemed fit to attend, so I had to leave Prince Phillip and the comfortable, safe world of deaf ed behind.

Elementary school started with my mother sending a note to my teacher explaining that I wore hearing aids and would need to sit in the front of the class. It also said that I might require some extra help. At this school, I still took speech therapy; the speech therapist would take me out of class to work with me. However, I didn't study sign language anymore. I didn't have any friends who knew how to sign, and my parents hadn't learned, so I gradually forgot what I'd learned in deaf ed. I became proficient at reading lips and watching people intently to get by.

I also became a voracious reader. Learning to read at a young age, I grew to love books; and I loved immersing myself in stories. I enjoyed a wide variety of material early on; but as I got older, my tastes turned mostly toward biographies and fiction. I loved reading about people in different places and about their cultures, traditions, and home lives. I found myself becoming so involved in the characters' worlds that I was always sad when I finished a book and it was over—it felt like a relationship ended. I could finish a book in a matter of hours. I even spent all of my allowance buying books at garage sales. It got so ridiculous that my dad finally said one day that I could quit spending my allowance on books and that he'd buy them instead. I can remember my mom and dad sitting on my bed with me at night when I was young, reading books and working with me on pronunciation. They would teach me to watch their mouths and pay attention to their teeth placement, the way their lips moved as they said a certain word, and where they put their tongue. One night, according to my dad, I took a book from him and said, "Here, Dad.

I'll read." He was shocked that I was able to read *him* a
story. From then on, I did most of the bedtime reading.

While I loved reading, I was also a big talker—so
much so that my report cards were always a conundrum.
I'd have straight A's (or close to it), but you know that
part on the report card that has check marks for certain
areas you didn't do well in? Well, it never failed; I'd
always fill up any section that related to talking in class
or not paying attention. My dad and even my grandpa
would make jokes about having to send me to school
with duct tape on my mouth. Thankfully, they never
actually did it.

Early on in elementary school, my classmates didn't
seem to notice things like skin color, age, gender, or the
fact that I ignored or didn't hear much of what they
said. They just wanted to play, so they made friends with
anyone who'd team up with them on the playground.
Later, though, the taunting started. Not being able
to pick up on most things that were said, and being

thought of as "dumb" because I didn't respond to things I couldn't hear, made me an easy target. I was lucky that it was never too intense or lasted too long—or maybe I just blocked it out or didn't catch most of it.

I do remember one time when I fell on the playground and my hearing aid fell off. One of the little boys on the playground ran over to me and stomped on it. I remember being so scared and worried about telling my parents. (Naturally, they didn't get angry at me; they were just angry about the situation I'd been put in.) My older hearing aids stuck out like a sore thumb and were a bull's-eye for some kids' jokes. I'm not sure why, but it was mostly boys who were cruel. Regardless of the taunting, I was a happy-go-lucky kid. That, combined with my parents' effort to always lift me up and affirm me, helped me get through childhood. As a parent myself now, I cannot imagine the anguish I'd experience if either of my girls were bullied in the manner that I was. My heart breaks for children with disabilities—and even children who simply wear glasses or braces and get made fun of by their classmates. Part of me wants to be that crazy mom who starts spanking other kids or stands up for a complete stranger's kid on the playground. However, I know by looking back on my own life, my experiences became a part of me, just the same as it does for everyone else. Those "lessons" help make all of us who we are and teach us how to process and cope with the world as we grow.

As I grew into adulthood, I found high school to be a painful experience at times. In elementary school, kids can be mean. By the time they reach high school though, those same kids can be just plain cruel. I'm not sure if it's all the hormones screaming through a teen's body or if it's just an age where they're trying out their independence and finding their way in the world, but navigating through high school is tough. On top of just trying to focus on school, I was going through so many changes and experiencing so much at this time. To cope,

I learned to feed off the people around me. If someone was laughing, I laughed. If someone seemed offended, I acted offended. If someone made a rude remark, I joined in. Everyday socializing was tricky enough for me; but on top of that, I wanted boys to notice me. Trying to impress a guy at the age of fourteen is painful enough when you're scrawny, you have acne, your hair doesn't cooperate with you, and you're worried about not having the right clothes. Add hearing aids to the mix, and that really scatters 'em.

There was one unpleasant high school experience that I remember vividly. It was a Friday afternoon, and my friends and I were on the bus heading home to get ready for a football game. There was a girl on the bus who was essentially known as the bus bully. She was a grade above me, bigger than me, and very outspoken. I had attended school with her for years and had often endured her taunting and ugly behavior—not just toward me, but toward others as well. At one point, she started picking on a friend of mine, teasing her because she was dating my friend's ex-boyfriend. I'm not sure what came over me—if it was the wind in my hair and feeling frisky because the weekend was upon us or if I just had a moment of insanity. Whatever the reason, I told her to shut up and stop picking on my friend. It quickly escalated into a standing-up, facing-each-other showdown. She was not happy about being told to shut up, so she responded by calling me a "deaf bitch."

I have to say that what happened next was like watching myself from outside myself—like being removed from my body and just floating around, watching the events unfold. I have said many times over the years while telling this story that it was like watching my fist do all of the work. As soon as the girl spoke the words "deaf bitch," I popped her hard with my fist— right square in the mouth. Because she wore braces, she started bleeding immediately. What ensued was a bit of a blur, but I know we fell onto the lap of a fellow bus rider.

At one point, she went for my ears, and angry red flashed through my vision. I released years of pent up hurt and anger; I went to town, just punching at whatever my fists made contact with. Eventually, someone pulled the girl off me, and we were separated. She was hunched over, spitting up blood, and I was made to sit at the front of the bus. I smiled like a crazy person the whole way home. To this day, I'm still not sure why the bus driver didn't call the cops or write us up.

When I got home, I had to tell my parents what happened. I was a bit concerned that I'd get into trouble for fighting and actually throwing the first punch. My parents had taught me to never lay my hands on anyone in anger. (And I'd like to add that I've never believed— and still don't believe—that fighting solves anything.) However, once my dad heard what caused me to react the way I did, I swear he smiled and got a twinkle in his eye. I think it occurred to him then that I'd be okay— that I could defend myself if need be and wouldn't let myself be pushed around. Looking back, I think prior to that incident he had worried about me. In that moment, I grew up a little.

During my last couple of years in high school, I yearned for some sense of responsibility. I wanted badly to interact in the "adult world." I had this preconceived notion that adults were all grown up. I just assumed that they would be more respectful, have more manners, and be more kind and mature. I also wanted money to spend on things, and I was excited by the prospect of having some independence. In our small town, a café had recently opened up; and one night while eating there, the owner came to our table to apologize for the slow service. He mentioned that he was short-handed and struggling to serve everyone in a timely fashion. I don't remember if he asked or if I did, but the opportunity for me to work there was brought up. I immediately began begging my dad to let me get the job, assuring him I could do it and really wanted to. I don't know if my deafness and wearing hearing aids had anything to do with his reluctance or if it was my being his only child that made it hard for him to swallow, but I really had to beg. It worked! I started just a couple of days later.

Working in the food industry was fun. I often joke that if it paid better, I'd still be waiting tables somewhere. I got along great with my boss, who had a thick Italian accent; he'd make fun of me for not hearing well, and I'd make fun of him for not forming his words properly. People would come and go, and I even developed relationships with some folks I saw regularly. I was always quick to explain to most customers that I wore hearing aids and read lips and that I'd need them to please be patient with me. In spite of being deaf, I was a great waitress. I moved fast; I memorized orders; I never left anyone wanting for anything; and I paid close attention to the details. This got me through the job, and I rarely got a complaint. I watched my customers interact with their families and friends and learned a lot about society and relationships. Most people were extremely understanding and kind.

There was one particular occasion, however, when I learned the hard way that even grown people can sometimes be jerks. A man came in who had a mustache, spoke low, didn't look at me, and mumbled—a deaf person's WORST nightmare! My routine with folks like this was always the same. I'd start out by saying "I'm sorry, what did you say?" then onto "What was that again please?" Then, in dire circumstances, I'd bust out the ol' "I wear hearing aids and read lips. Could you please repeat that and look at me?" But before I could get to step three, this particular man snapped at me, "What are you, deaf or something?!?" At this point, I explained to him, embarrassed and bright red, that yes, in fact, I *was* deaf. I pulled my hair back and pointed to my hearing aids for emphasis. The man looked me square in the eye and said, "Well, how am I supposed to know that? You should wear a sign around your neck or something!" I walked away with tears streaming down my face and went into the kitchen to cry. Another waitress overheard what happened and took the table from me.

As I said, I learned a lot about life, the world, and society from that job. I got my nose bloodied so-to-speak, but most of my experiences at the café were positive. And on a particularly good note, it was there that I met the man who would eventually become my husband.

All things considered, my life growing up was great. My parents were superb at never letting me feel sorry for myself and never letting me get down. They gave me affirmation and assured me that I could try anything in the world. I enjoyed my youth and appreciated my family's support so deeply that it was only in secret that I would contemplate what I was missing—what my world would be like with sound.

Three

Growing up, I became keenly aware that I was missing out on some simple but meaningful aspects of everyday life that folks with hearing naturally take for granted.

As a child, a major rite of passage for a little girl is sleepovers. A bunch of girls crammed into a living room with sleeping bags, board games, and popcorn is a staple in every young girl's life. Staying up late and gossiping, telling secrets, and giggling. I was in love with these nights as much as any other child. A few things always made it difficult though. There was always a girl in the group who would start making fun of me or questioning why I wore hearing aids, why I took them out at night, and what was the little jar I kept them in. (I had a jar partially filled with desiccant beads that dried the moisture out of my hearing aids at night.) But those things didn't bother me as much as missing out on telling secrets or whispering in the dark at night and being able to giggle along with all the other girls. At a young age, missing out on who had a crush on the cute boy in our gym class and what the class bully said on the playground were important pieces of information that I often wasn't clued in on.

You see, once the lights were off, I couldn't see anyone's lips, so I couldn't read them. While my friends would stay up talking, giggling, and telling secrets, I'd be lying there with tears in my eyes because I couldn't join in. For whatever reason, I was too embarrassed or shy to admit that I was not getting what was said. Out of shame, I rarely asked for them to repeat what they were talking about. I either tried to seem cool, like I was totally involved in the conversation, or I just pretended I had fallen asleep.

Kids just aren't empathetic and don't think of others' feelings the way adults often do. I don't think any of my friends ever took the time to put themselves in my shoes until they were older. I also think that most of my friends never really understood just how difficult life was for me. They didn't realize how hard I worked on a daily basis to fit in and get along. I don't say this to make anyone feel sorry for me, and I tried to never feel sorry for myself for too long. When life was tough or my day at school was hard or I had a rough night at a sleepover, I knew the sun would come up the next morning and a new day would start. I could enjoy my friends all over again.

Even as an adult, I was still unable to interact or be involved in social settings the way I really desired. Everything from going out to eat with friends to attending family functions was a missed opportunity. Family parties were always tough for me, especially holiday parties where everyone gathered and talked about things going on in their lives. I didn't catch the little jokes that Uncle Jack told or the story my cousin Leslie was cracking everyone up with. I missed out on the latest information about who was pregnant or who was getting married. As a kid, it wasn't that important to me because all I wanted to do was run around with the other kids and play. But as I got older, I wanted to be involved in the grown-up chatter. I wanted to be able to talk about my own life and listen to others the way everyone else did.

It wasn't just the wide gaps in social interactions that frustrated me; it was the smaller things too. People always talked about how much they enjoyed hearing raindrops on the roof or just sitting on the porch listening to a storm. If I saw that it was raining heavily, sometimes I would step outside and try to figure out if I was actually hearing something or simply *feeling* it. Vibrations are everything to a deaf person; we rely on them to get by. If the rain was loud enough, sometimes some sound would sneak through, but it would be distorted and muffled—almost like the sound of static on a TV. Even with hearing aids, I couldn't hear the rain like everyone else, and the romanticized concept of it seemed incomplete to me because I could only see and feel it.

Television and movies were another source of frustration since closed captioning didn't come along until I was an older kid. For most of my childhood, I simply watched the images on television. If I turned the sound up really loudly, I could hear some sort of noise, but I couldn't distinguish words or specific sounds. When I went to movie theaters, the huge screens made reading the actors' lips fairly easy as long as the shot included a good view of the speaker's face. Unfortunately though, I'd miss out on most of the dialogue, the sound effects, and the tone of what was being spoken, so the movie as a whole wouldn't make sense. I always had to have someone explain to me what was going on, or I'd just wait until the movie was over and ask, "Okay, what was that about?" Thankfully, as I got older, the use of closed captioning on television became more widespread. Some theaters began using it as well, although such screenings were, and still are, limited to specific weekday matinees.

"Listening" to the radio was an adventure all its own. I couldn't understand any of the content or advertisements being spoken, so I'd just wait until the station played music and then crank my stereo up. This has always been hard for me to explain, but even though I couldn't make out the lyrics to a song or even what instruments were being played, I still enjoyed music in my own way. I could feel the beat, and I'd make up lyrics in my head if I didn't know the song.

As a child, I remember being in the car with my parents when they'd let me turn the radio up loud. Every once in a while, they'd catch me singing and say, "What did you say?" or "What do you think they're saying?"

I'd have to explain that I just made up lyrics and words in my head to go along with the beat I felt. I had some pretty funny ones and some weird ones too. My parents and my friends always got a kick out of the lyrics I made up for popular songs. Even now that I can hear words to music, I still find myself singing the "old" lyrics I grew up singing.

Sometimes, though, I would take the time to actually learn a song the right way. I'd look at the cassette tape liner notes and read the lyrics, or I'd have someone tell me what they were. As I got older and the Internet became available, I'd Google the lyrics. I would write them down and read them several times until I'd memorized them. Then I'd play the music loudly over and over until I had created the song in my head.

Once I was old enough to drive, I was in heaven. I'd crank that radio up and blast music while cruising down the road. I learned that if I turned the bass all the way up, I could really feel it. When my dad would get in my truck, he would try to "fix" all my stereo settings. He'd say, "This sounds AWFUL! Let me fix it for you." I never knew the difference; I just liked it loud so I could enjoy it. Driving down the road with my stereo blasting out of balance, windows down, and the wind blowing through my hair are some of my favorite memories. I didn't have to worry about hurting anyone else's ears. I didn't care about the fact that the bass was all out of whack or that I was singing along at the top of my lungs, way out of tune, to made-up lyrics. I even blew the speakers out in my old truck once! Sometimes, my mom would let me drive her cool Trans-Am to school, and I was instructed not to mess with any of the radio settings or take the t-tops out until after school. Obviously, I didn't listen. I'd pull out of my neighborhood, pull over, take the tops off, crank up the stereo, and cruise to school in style.

There were other sounds I longed for in my first twenty-seven years. My long list made short would involve sounds like hearing birds outside, engines in cars, someone knocking at the door, the microwave going off, and even picking up on sarcasm and jokes that relied on tone. People don't often stop to think about how important tone is. Tone is everything in language. You can say the same sentence in three different tones, and it can be taken three different ways. I can recall instances that I got my feelings hurt because of something that was said, and then I'd get made fun of for being upset. People would think, "What is she upset for? She's a cry baby." What they didn't realize, though, is that I couldn't distinguish the tone. I couldn't understand that what was said wasn't actually meant to be mean or ugly. For example, someone would say something like, "You're funny," and mean it genuinely, but I'd think they were being snarky.

On the other hand, there were times when someone would say something cruel, but I didn't realize it. Someone on the bus or in the hallway might have said something nasty; but if they said it while smiling, I would've just smiled back and gone about my business. If someone said, "Sure, that happened" with a sarcastic tone, it'd take another person bringing it to my attention for me to realize that it was rude. Sarcasm and dry humor are often lost on the deaf community. Unless I knew someone well, I never knew how to read them. I have an uncle named Harold who has a very dry, sarcastic humor. He'd make jokes and do it all without a smile, and I'd be so lost. I remember several times he made me cry because he'd tell a joke and I wouldn't get it, and then he'd poke fun at me, resulting in my feelings being hurt. I tried my hardest as a child to avoid him at family parties. It was only as I got older that I realized he and some other folks in the family just had what was called "dry humor." Growing up, I was naïve and just assumed that if someone looked nice, or smiled, they were being nice—that's not always the case, unfortunately.

My greatest challenge with tone came in 2006
when I attempted to learn Mandarin. My husband and I
had moved to China for a mission trip where he taught
English at a university for a year. Part of the job involved
taking classes to learn Mandarin, which is very much a
tonal language. The same *word* can be pronounced three
different ways and have three *very* different meanings.
It was impossible for me to learn the language well
because I couldn't pick up on the tones. I learned some
key phrases; and with my Southern accent along with my
charades, I could manage. But I never went anywhere or
did any kind of errand or shopping without my husband
or a friend in tow. It was one of the most challenging
years of my life for many reasons, but the language was
a big part of it. However, not knowing the language well
caused me to really take in all that went on around me. I
realized that I as long as I could smile, all would be well,
just like so many other times in my life. Even in a foreign
land, I learned how far just a smile would truly get me.

Powered On

I could go on and on about the small things
I missed out on, but being deaf for most of my life
allowed me to gain a unique perspective on the world.
People often focus on the big things and miss out on
so much—a bird singing in the trees, the leaves rustling
on the ground, acorns falling, a child's laughter, and so
much more. These were all sounds I wanted so badly
to be able to appreciate but couldn't. I kind of look at
myself as a proverbial gardener. Much of the world
typically focuses on what fruits and vegetables they
can get from a garden—what sustenance it can provide
them, what joy they can get from it, or how it can
benefit them. Seldom do folks realize that the small
actions like pulling weeds and watering the garden are
what actually produce the bounty. The garden cannot
flourish or produce unless these small things are done.
When I was deaf, the small details were my world—I
always lived in the moment. My life has really been
cracked wide open recently, but I hope to not become so

immersed in it that I forget to pay attention to the small things and take nothing for granted. While my identity was never in my deafness, I hope that I never lose what I actually gained from being deaf and focusing inward for so long.

Four

I've always been a glass-half-full kind of gal. For me,
being deaf was just the way my life was—it was all I had
ever known. I have always found my identity through
my relationships and in my connection with others.
I've always worked hard to be a great daughter, friend,
wife, and mother. Growing up deaf never defined me as
a person, and my world most definitely didn't revolve
around my deafness.

In fact, I was twenty-one years old before I learned
that I was considered disabled in the eyes of society.
I've always had a great love for animals, and I grew up

with many pets. I really wanted to work with animals in some capacity; and eventually, I was offered a job at a friend's grooming shop. It was just a front desk job; but while I worked there, I decided I wanted to become a dog groomer. The owner, Lee, was a kind lady and was willing to teach me some, but she was busy running a shop. She suggested I look into grooming schools, and I later found one in my area. Upon speaking with the staff, I learned that the Texas Rehabilitation Center might pay for my schooling because I was "disabled." I thought, "I'm disabled?"

Suddenly, I found myself undergoing hearing tests, IQ tests, personality assessments, and other random tests to see if I qualified for disability aid. It was amazing to me. I sat in the office after the testing, and I was stunned. I had never in my life thought of myself as having a disability. My mom and dad had never raised me or treated me as if I were disabled. They only built me up, socialized me, treated me "normal," and boosted my self-esteem.

They always told me I could try anything I wanted. That didn't mean that I would necessarily *succeed* at everything, but I could always *try*. I remember one time they let me try out for the basketball team. They paid the money for me to get a physical, and they even put up a goal at the house for me to shoot hoops with. Even though they knew full well that I was horrible with a ball, they supported me and were never negative. Of course, I didn't even come close to making the team; but as an adult, I look back on that, and I'm touched that they never stopped me from trying. As a kid, it's so important to have parents who are constantly building you up, whether you have a disability or not.

As I've mentioned already, it wasn't all bad being deaf. I have to admit that there were actually some good aspects. I was confronted with many challenges along the way, and I learned when you can't always tune into the world around you, you tend to turn inside yourself somewhat. Imagine putting in a pair of really good ear plugs for a day and not having any way to take them out. Once you overcome the initial frustration, imagine all the time you'd have to think about life and go over things in your head without all the distractions around you. Like I said, I tend to evaluate settings around me and pay attention to minute details like the paint peeling on the wall, the cobweb in the corner, the picture that is a little crooked, or a crack in the concrete—lots of small things that are usually overlooked. I also think deeply about the lives and emotions of the people around me.

So imagine that day with ear plugs turning into weeks or months—you'd still have to function, right? Over time, you'd begin to notice and pay attention to body language and demeanors. You'd start to focus on faces—not just to read lips, but to look at people's eyes and *in* their eyes. When you become so dependent on interpreting a person's face in order to truly converse, you really begin to pick up on how people look when they are angry, sad, happy, or even lying.

It's similar to reading those gossip magazines at the news stand—the ones that have pictures of a famous couple and the headline reads "Brad and Angelina are done!" You open up the paper, look at the article, and see a picture of Brad Pitt and Angelina Jolie. They're standing apart from each other, one person's body turned slightly away, and maybe Angelina's hands are folded across her body. Brad's eyebrows are furrowed, and Angelina's lips are pouted. The article then goes on to tell you that some famous body language expert has determined from the photograph that the lovely couple is done. The body language expert was probably right that there was tension between them, but what the "expert" fails to point out or grasp is that it was just one small *moment* in their lives while they were in the middle of a simple argument. I've been a "moment-to-moment" body language expert in my daily life for twenty-nine years.

I'm also quite the skilled lip reader. One time when I was a small child, I was out with my parents in public, and I saw a grown couple having a quiet fight. I leaned over and asked my mom, "What is a bastard?" She immediately said, "Where did you hear that?!?" I had read the couple's lips and "listened" to their fight. My dad thought it was particularly funny if we were out somewhere and there seemed to be a great conversation going on. He'd lean over and say, "What are they talking about?" Some conversations were more interesting than others, of course. On one such occasion, I remember "listening" to two old ladies arguing over how to cook a Thanksgiving turkey at the bingo hall. Exciting night at the bingo hall!

I can remember in middle school sitting at the lunch table with my friend Samantha. A group of

girls were a few tables away, and I noticed that they
were looking at us kind of funny, so I pointed it out to
Samantha. She asked me what they were talking about,
so I started reading their lips. Sadly, they were talking
about her and saying some not-so-nice things. Now, this
is the part where I should explain that I'm a horrible liar;
I've never been able to look someone in the face and lie.
When Samantha asked what the girls at the other table
were saying, I knew she wouldn't believe me if I tried
to lie about it, so I told her the truth. The funny part is
that when lunch was over and we were in the hallway
heading back to class, Sam walked over to the girls and
told them off. She repeated the ugly words they had
said about her, and the looks on those girls' faces were
priceless. They asked her how she knew what they had
said, and I'll never forget her answer. She said, "I have
my ways."

Another attribute that can be gained from being
"inside" yourself is that you start to really focus on your

surroundings and pay attention to the chain of events in certain situations. In a way, you begin to spot events before they happen. Without audible distractions, you focus more on things others don't see. For instance, I could be at the park, watching all the kiddos running around and playing and the moms chatting. I might see a group of kids huddle together and head over to a slide. Meanwhile, a toddler might be making his way toward the bottom of the slide as one of the bigger kids is preparing for take-off. In situations like these, I could shout at one of the mothers or run over and grab the little one in time to avoid a collision.

We've all seen this type of scene depicted in movies, and it's a lot like what I've experienced. Maybe it takes place in a busy subway with people rushing all around. The movie cuts to one of the main characters in the crowd, and that character stands completely still, looking around, while hundreds of folks rush to and fro. Babies are crying, the train is coming through the station, and there is the appearance of incredibly loud noise and chatter, but the scene is quiet, capturing the character's internal focus. That is the best way I can describe it. It's an ability to just shut out the world and focus on situations around you.

I believe my years without hearing also instilled in me a heightened sense of empathy. Some of it may just be my personality or nature, but I think a large part has to do with the fact that I do pay such close attention to faces and emotions. Sitting across the room from someone watching their face crumble, as they begin to cry after receiving what is obviously bad news, is utterly heartbreaking to me. I catch myself almost making the same face and then feeling so sorry and sad for them. Watching people in pain really gets to me too. I can remember when my husband, Sloan, had to be rushed to the hospital because his thumb was cut off in an accident involving a tractor. I was nine months pregnant and due any day with our first child when I got the call that Sloan had been taken to the ER. I rushed there; and when I arrived, he was in extreme pain and holding his hand as the nurses and doctor frantically prepped him for surgery. I was fine being there and watching him until the doctor came back in with a needle and said he'd need to give Sloan several shots directly into the raw meat of his thumb. Now, I've never had a problem with shots or needles or blood, but watching them prick those needles into the raw part of his thumb and watching his face in utter agony was just too much for me. It's the one time in my life that I've walked away when someone was in pain. I felt horrible as I stood in the hallway while they administered the shots; but when I returned to Sloan's side, I explained that I just could not watch him. Thankfully, he understood.

Clearly, being so sensitive and in tune didn't always work out in my favor. Several times throughout the years, I had to get new hearing aids, and I dreaded it every time. After spending so much time getting comfortable with an old set and the sounds I was used to hearing, getting new hearing aids was frustrating. Even though I'd be upgrading to a pair that worked better or better suited me and my needs, it just rocked my world terribly. Adjusting to the new hearing aids and all the changes they brought was mentally exhausting, and getting used to the new buzz, hum, and distortion every time just depressed me. [I should probably explain that hearing aids do not give natural hearing; it's mechanical. Because of that, there is always a constant hum or roar, kind of like white noise. They raise the volume of everything to the same level. That, along with the noise the hearing aids produce, can make certain situations maddening.] As I got older, I started learning to take the changes a bit more in stride. I started realizing that everything went much smoother if I just focused on the positive aspects of each situation.

My whole life has been spent essentially turning lemons into lemonade; I've always just done the best with what I had. I have felt in my heart from a young age that God had a plan for me and I've just spent my life trusting that at some point, I'd realize I was walking out that plan. I've always been able to face a problem head-on and just trust that life would work out for the better in the end. Sometimes that belief takes realizing that I may not know why things happen but that I need to just accept it and trust in God.

People often say "God will not give you more than you can handle," but I don't believe that's quite right. God *may* give you more than you think you can handle, but He will also give you the tools to get through those tough times. Challenges are what mold us and shape us into who we are. I've never thought God gave me too much to handle; I've looked at it as if He's given me a chance to become a unique person. He's given me the tools to have some very desirable qualities. He's also given me the opportunity to meet people and go places I never thought I would. That's how I look at my life and the struggles in it. Everyone is going through something in life, and it may not always be obvious what the person's struggles are. Some people may be expecting big answers in this book, but I'm content with the idea that maybe I went through the challenges I faced to show just *one* person that there's more to life than the obstacles he or she is struggling with, whatever those obstacles may be.

Five

In life, we are all faced with situations where we should be bold enough to speak up about something going on, or at least stand up for ourselves. I'd love to say I did everything all on my own; but the truth is that I learned, over time, that it's important to have someone who has your back—someone who will build you up daily.

People face social struggles throughout their lives for many different reasons. For me, these started to become evident as I entered my teen years. In a lot of ways, high school was very much a painful time in my life, as it was for many kids. While some teens

were worried about their weight, their grades, the
neighborhood they lived in, or what car they drove,
I was more worried about my not-so-perfect ears.

There was one unsettling incident on the bus that
I remember vividly. Because of the noise and chaos and
my lack of hearing, I was rarely able to keep up and read
lips; if I did, it was tiresome. This made it hard for me
to stand up for myself or anyone else in most situations
because I'd miss whole conversations—or at least miss
enough that I wasn't completely aware of what was
going on or being said. This particular day, I was sitting
in front of this older guy who was making fun of me for
something unrelated to my hearing aids. It started before
we got on the bus, and I knew it would continue once
we got on. But I just chose to ignore him and not even
turn around and attempt to read his lips or try to keep up
with what he was saying. I honestly felt like ignoring him
was the best thing to do. That didn't work out so well; he
apparently kept hurling insults. Those insults turned into

insults about my not hearing him, which then led to him throwing things at me. Random stuff began hitting me: pencils, pens, paper—nothing major, so I just continued to ignore him. It was all I could think to do since I had no idea what he was saying and I wasn't brave enough to say anything back to him or ask him to leave me alone. Ignoring him, however, only made him angrier.

According to those around me who told me later, he spouted off something rude about my hearing aids; and the next thing I knew, he punched me in the head. Honestly, it didn't hurt all that bad; I was just shocked that a guy actually punched me. Something about the opposite sex picking on me and getting physical with me was such a helpless feeling. He was a guy—I was no match for him. So as I sat there in shock, I began to cry because I was so embarrassed. I wondered what those around me thought. In my mind, I was figuring they probably thought I was dumb. Thankfully, the bus pulled up to campus almost immediately after the incident, and

I was able to get off and run away from everyone. That's just one example of how my not standing up for myself or those around me escalated into something bigger. All it would have probably taken was me asking him to leave me alone or someone else standing up for me. As the end of the school year neared, I was starting to really look forward to graduating and getting more into the "adult world."

As I mentioned earlier, I learned the hard way that the "adult world" could be just as challenging. But I also learned that I didn't have to face it alone.

I was seventeen when I met Sloan. His parents came into the café to eat pretty regularly, and I grew fond of them. As I discovered later, they had been telling their son about me. Sloan came in one night after seeing me on a previous dinner visit. As he walked in the door, I handed him a menu. He said to me, "I don't want a menu; I'd like your phone number." Later that night, I told my mom, "I just met the man I'm going to marry."

After Sloan asked me out at the café, we saw each other every day until we got married nearly two years later on November 17, 2001. I had just turned nineteen and had graduated from high school, and Sloan was twenty-one. During those two years of courtship, Sloan became the reason I blossomed. He was always there to encourage me in any new endeavor and also to be a shoulder to cry on when things didn't go so well. He gave me confidence I didn't know I had and always stepped back and let me do things as if there were no boundaries, no limitations. He still lifts me up daily, and I am the woman I am today because of him. He has spent the last thirteen years being my translator and interpreter in life, and I really feel like that has made us closer than some other couples. I allowed myself to depend on someone who really loves me.

Over the years, we had developed a routine that was not noticeable to most—a series of touches on my hand to let me know in a crowded atmosphere at a party that he'd tell me what everyone was saying in just a moment or a brush against my leg to let me know that I was interrupting someone. He'd always lean over, look me in the eyes, and silently repeat what had been said when he knew I hadn't gotten it. He was quick to explain to me what someone said when he realized I hadn't understood the question. He always did it in a manner that was kind and never embarrassed me; and much of the time, he acted like he was the one who was confused, just to take the attention off of me. Sloan even learned to lip read, and we'd have silent conversations from across the room at a crowded parties. We call it "lipping," and throughout our relationship, we have "lipped" at each other while at functions to see if the other was ready to go, to check in, or just to connect in our own private way.

Sloan's graceful social assists even continued when we were alone. On the way home from social events and family functions, he was always considerate and patient about filling me in on anything I might have missed. We'd have a debriefing in the car to explain things like who was that lady with Cousin Tyler or what was wrong with Aunt Shirley. I felt so much more connected with Sloan by my side.

Through the years, we've learned about life and grown together. There was a time in our marriage when Sloan developed a love for motorcycles. He'd get his hands on one and do all sorts of modifications to make it faster, lighter, etc. Eventually, he decided he wanted to build a customized motorcycle from the ground up, but first, he wanted to spend a day with my grandfather, Bobby Langley. My grandpa was a big drag racer back in the late 50's and 60's. He is in the hall of fame, and he was a master craftsman in many areas. He had built his own race cars and was very knowledgeable about the mechanics of building something from scratch. So Sloan blocked out a whole afternoon to go and bask in my grandpa's knowledge. I remember him saying that he wanted to go "soak up all he could, like a sponge." He was only gone an hour, and when he returned, I asked what happened. Sloan told me that all my grandpa had to tell him was, "Just try it; if it don't work, start over and try again." At the time, that infuriated Sloan; but as he got older and spent many more years building bikes, he came to realize how valuable that information was and how foolish it was to be so upset with grandpa. We found humor in the memory, and it became our one-liner joke: "Just try it; if it don't work, start over and try again." We sort of adopted it as a can-do philosophy.

It was after the mission trip we took together to China in 2007, however, that we really changed the way we approached life. When we returned, everyone's number-one question was always, "Did you experience culture shock?" Sloan and I were always quick to explain that the culture shock upon arriving back home was worse. We realized after living abroad for a year that America is consumed with the nine-to-five,

keeping-up-with-the-Joneses, materialistic way of life.
It broke our hearts to see this attitude all around us and
realize that we ourselves had gotten caught up in it a bit.

Understanding the dangers of materialism
became our greatest lesson. We began to really value
relationships and came to realize how important love
and family and good friends are. We realized the value of
spending time with people and enjoying just the simple
things. We wanted to start giving people in our lives our
all because we finally understood that you only have this
time for so long. The grass can be mowed tomorrow, and
the car can be washed next week—get your cable shut
off and make memories with your loved ones.

Growing up deaf, I was forced to stay in the
present moment and to give my full attention to those
I was spending time with. These actions have grown
into qualities that I hope to never lose and that I hope
will stay with me the remainder of my days. I see these
good qualities as ways God allowed me to be a unique

person with a unique outlook on life. I think God has given all of us our own unique qualities—it's just up to us to use them and appreciate them. It's up to us to look past what the world may see as a "disability" and find the good aspects in our lives. That whole "making lemonade out of lemons" thing comes in handy for finding the positive and has been a very important reminder to our family about how to be truly happy.

Six

I've been reminded many times in my life that when you leave this earth, you can't take material possessions with you. As I've grown older and gotten a family of my own, I've come to realize how important that statement is. Many times when I've wanted things that weren't sensible or necessary, I've had to remind myself of this saying. For instance, not tying myself down to a monthly car payment might allow me to pay for my daughters to take dance lessons and gymnastics. It might also allow Sloan and I to take our girls to movies, on more weekend trips, etc. We'd rather make memories and spend time with each other, our kids, our family, and our friends. I've thought about all this often, and it has led me to ask myself and others:

"Are YOU happy?"

About three years ago, we really started going through a rough spell in our lives. We lost a baby when our older daughter Olivia Li was one. I was literally miscarrying at her first birthday party, a time when friends and family were all gathered to celebrate a happy occasion. We also buried several family members. All five of our dogs died, and we lost cattle and horses. (My husband and in-laws have had horses and cattle for years. They rope calves and steers, and train horses off and on, and we raise beef cattle.) We had stuff stolen, and there was an attempted break in at my mother-in-law's house. Cars and tractors were breaking down, my husband was out of work, we were in a drought, and our pastures were dying. It just seemed as if nothing could go right. A new year was around the corner, but little did we know that the worst was yet to come.

When January arrived, it brought with it our most difficult battle. My grandfather-in-law passed away on January 8th. We buried him that Saturday. Just days later, on Wednesday the 14th, my father in-law, Ross Churman, passed away suddenly. He was buried the following Saturday. My mother in-law had to bury her father and her husband within a week's time. As a family, we were all absolutely devastated.

My father in-law was an amazing man and a very important figure in my family's lives. He was who we went to for wisdom and for prayer when life was tough. He was the person who had the most impact on me in my walk with God. He showed me the love of the Father through his actions. He was a giver; he'd give his last dollar to someone if he felt led, and he wouldn't worry about where he'd get more money to pay the next bill. He always just trusted in God and trusted that by doing what he felt led to do, he'd be taken care of. I never saw him let his anger get the best of him. In a situation in which someone was rude or said something offensive that would get most other people angry, he would just walk away or remain calm. It was very admirable.

I can remember a time that I was wrongly fired from a job. My boss had not been honest with me about my employment, and a client spilled the beans that he was only keeping me around until a former employee returned back to work. When I confronted him about it, he yelled at me and told me I was fired and to "get the hell out of his office." I can remember that I couldn't get a hold of Sloan, so I called Ross. He promptly showed up to help me pack up all my belongings. I'll never forget; he just hugged me and prayed for me in the middle of my office.

He also taught me patience and to not let my flesh or my greed make an important decision. Sloan and I were married young, and we had a tendency to get excited about buying a car or making a big purchase.

We'd ask Ross for his wisdom, and he'd always say things like, "Take a few days to pray and think about it. If it's meant to be, it will happen. It will work itself out." Being young and anxious, his advice is not what we always wanted to hear—but now, years later, I look back on all that he told us and still follow those suggestions and greatly appreciate them. He always had simple words of wisdom for the tough times we went through. He was a quiet man for the most part; but when he did speak, everyone listened.

Ross rode cutting horses, trained calf-roping horses, and taught kids how to rope for most of his life. He was a well-known guy in the horse world and was well respected by many. I actually met Ross first before I met Sloan. He had a kind spirit and had a way of sharing God's love with few words. It's hard to explain, but there was just a peace about him; and those who came in contact with him just knew there was something special about him.

He was a man who was admired by so many. The reason he was so well-liked was evident in something that was said to me after he died that I'll never forget: "He was the only person I knew who actually 'walked the walk,' and being around him made me want to be a better person." What an awesome thing to say about someone!

With Ross gone, it left a huge void in our lives; but three weeks after his passing, my youngest daughter Elise An was born. She was the extremely bright silver lining to our dark cloud. I gave birth to her at home surrounded by six midwives, both of my moms, an aunt, a cousin who photographed the whole birth, my oldest daughter Olivia, and Sloan. It was a surreal experience for Sloan and me and brought us so much joy. It was during this time that we really began to look back on our lives and all we had experienced.

Losing Ross made us appreciate so much, the most important being love and relationships. We really had a "light bulb moment" and realized that our most fond memories—the memories that had shaped us into who we were as people—all occurred around family and friends and the time spent with them. Relationships were the common thread of our lives.

As I stated earlier, my identity was never in my deafness. It's also never been in what car I drive, how big my house is, or how much money is in my bank account. Maybe you feel as if you have to have the newest phone or the nicest car, etc. What would happen if you just saved your money, remained satisfied with your old car and old phone, and took time off to spend it with family? I can promise you that your kids couldn't care less about whether or not a sports car is in your garage; they'd rather go on a vacation with Mom and Dad. Some of my fondest memories as a child were times spent at family lake houses, on road trips, or on vacations. I hope my children have many wonderful memories to look back on as they grow old. Would I like to have a nice shiny new vehicle that got more than fourteen miles to the gallon on diesel? Sure! But until I can afford one without being tied down to a monthly car payment, I am praising God for the truck I do have and the fact that it's paid for. I am happy with what I've got. What truly makes you happy? If you're honest with yourself, I'll bet it's your spouse, your kids, your siblings, your parents, and your friends.

With that being said, who do you surround yourself with? I'm almost thirty years old; and for the first twenty-eight years or so, I was not the best at ridding myself of toxic relationships. I've not always done well in surrounding myself with like-minded, positive people—people who want to be my friend just as much as I want to be theirs. When you surround yourself with people who constantly see the glass as half empty, your glass tends to become half empty over time. That whole concept of being a product of your environment is very true.

I used to work at a place where just about everyone was negative or unhappy. They talked behind each other's backs, griped and complained about everything, and put others down constantly. Of course, at the time, I couldn't see this negativity because my judgment was clouded from being around these people for hours each week. Once I left the place and looked back, I realized how unhappy everyone was. It was a learning opportunity.

One way that Sloan and I are so different is that he does not become attached to co-workers easily. He looks at his job as strictly a job; he's there to work and accomplish the day's tasks and not bond or mingle with folks. I, on the other hand, tend to bond with anyone I spend time with on a regular basis. It's burned me often in life, and I finally decided I wanted good friends—friends who bring just as much to the table as I do, friends who are able to pick up a phone or shoot an e-mail every so often to see how I'm doing.

Sloan and I both have started to recognize those relationships in which we're putting in a heck of a lot more than we're getting back. We've had to really consider who our true friends are. Sloan has often said of his dear friends, "They are the type of people I can call at three in the morning, and they'd help me chop up a body—no questions asked." Obviously, we aren't chopping up any bodies, but we are proud to say that our close true friends would come pick us up on the side of the road at midnight if our car broke down. We'd do the same for them as well. We also have let go of friendships when others didn't share our values. We have met people who were consumed with working non-stop and owning the biggest and best of everything; we've met people whose identity was in their job title and what they could do or what they could buy. I'm not saying there's anything wrong with owning a nice car, working 9 to 5, or being a millionaire. I'm just saying that it seems to me that people whose identities are wrapped up in jobs, money, and material items are the unhappiest folks I know. These types of friends started dragging us down, and we realized that we had to step away from them and focus on our true friends.

We aren't perfect; life is a constant learning process, and we make mistakes every so often. A relationship takes communication, and transparency is important as well. We try to be as transparent as possible with those we love, and we expect the same in return. It's kind of like searching for a husband or a wife; you have a certain set of expectations you want in a mate. A friendship should be the same way. Why not expect a lot? If you're willing to give a lot, you deserve a lot.

I have always worked so hard to get to know people and build relationships. I've given every friendship my all, and I've never taken one lightly. In the past, when I found someone who didn't care that I had hearing aids and was willing to spend the extra time and effort to communicate with me, I really became attached to them. When your way of communication involves having to focus on people intently as they talk, you find yourself really bonding. For me, speaking with someone was like isolating them from everything else around. I treated the people speaking as if they were the only one in the room, even when they weren't. All of my energy and emotion was invested in conversations and relationships.

I've tried to teach my girls to look at someone when speaking to them. I have always felt that it was such an endearing quality and that it's respectful. It makes people feel as if you really care about them, and I think it's a great attribute to have. It shows people you have nothing to hide. I was once told that an honest man will make eye contact with you. I want my girls to be honest people. People say you should treat others how you want to be treated; and if we're all honest with ourselves, we'd love for the people in our lives to give us their undivided attention. These days, everyone is so busy trying to do five things at once that not many take time to block out the busy world around them and focus on those they care for. I feel like if I can teach my girls anything, it's this.

Sloan and I do our best to instill our values in the girls. They spend so much time with grandparents, cousins, friends, etc. They attend dance lessons, gymnastics, Sunday school, camps, and more. We want them to be social but also particular about whom they befriend and get close to. We want them to value themselves enough to choose good people to surround themselves with. They'll spend so much of their lives with friends, making memories, and doing things that will leave impressions forever; these experiences should be with genuine folks who care about them—people who treasure life and those in it, and people who see the value in doing goofy things together. Things like having a picnic in the middle of the pasture using our great-grandmother's good china and laughing and just hanging out. I want them to find friends like my dear friend Misty, who sees opportunity in any situation. She can make a fun day out of perusing the local nursery with my kids in tow or going on a hike through our pastures, hunting for bugs or whatever kinds of animals we can find and taking pictures of them. She has a child-like desire for life and adventure, and that's something I don't mind rubbing off on me. When, at the age of thirty, you can go to the thrift store and try on the wackiest clothes and spend hours in the dressing rooms taking photos of hideous outfits and giggling hysterically, you know you've found a great friend. When I'm ninety-nine, I'll remember those moments the most.

Are *you* happy? As you look at all you do in life and who you spend time with, where are your priorities? Ask yourself, are you really, truly happy? That's what we should all take time to think about. I can say, at this point in my life, I AM HAPPY. I'm a twenty-nine-year-old woman with great friends and family, two incredible little girls, and a husband who adores me and is my rock. And, as you will soon learn, I'm living "born again" for the third time in my life with new ears.

Seven

I sort of fell between the cracks when it came to being deaf. I didn't fit the mold of a typical person with a hearing disability. As I've mentioned, when I attended deaf education school, I learned some of the basics of sign language; but I left that school early on and lost most of what I had been taught. My mom once said that she didn't learn sign because she didn't want to accept that I would have to use it. She was hopeful that I would not have to rely on it, and both my parents worked with me on speaking and reading lips. I was the half of the deaf culture that did not rely on sign, used my voice, and worked hard to integrate into society, wanting to be seen as what I considered to be "normal."

With that being said, I became fully aware of the other side of deafness as I grew older. I sometimes would meet a deaf person in public who relied solely on sign language, and I was reminded that there were those out there who had decided to turn their voice off, meaning they chose to not speak and to embrace sign language fully. I respect that choice. I realize that everyone is different and that everyone has a different view. For me, trying to talk and learning to read lips just made sense. There was never a time in my life when I didn't desire to hear fully. There was never a time when, if the chance were given to receive new ears, I wouldn't take it. I grew up just expecting that someday I'd be made fully whole. I clung to that. Quite frankly, maybe I was just too much of a nosy kid and hated to miss out on anything, and I just propelled myself and refused to be left behind. I wanted my voice to be heard.

As I've mentioned, for most of my life, I lived with the explanation that doctors had given my parents for my deafness. At twenty-one years old, I decided I wanted a better one. Sloan and I started seeing specialists to determine the root cause of my problem. I wanted a concrete answer; I wanted to know what was missing or what didn't work and if there was a way to fix it. After much testing and scanning, we found out that, in fact, I was missing most of the hairs in my ear. The hairs are what transmit the sound waves to the brain. It was just a genetic abnormality, not caused by medicine or any infection. It's just how I was made. At long last, I had the explanation I'd been looking for, but the solution was still not on the horizon.

In today's world, technology and provisions for the deaf and hard of hearing are still lagging. There aren't always interpreters available for those who sign, and society as a whole really isn't very aware of deaf culture. There's no way to provide every deaf person with an interpreter 24/7 so that they can attend school and work and lead an average life. Things as simple as ordering food in a drive-through aren't easily done and, in some instances, are flat-out impossible. The folks who choose to embrace sign language and rely on it solely have few provisions to accommodate them in their daily lives. I personally think this lack of progress is mostly because being deaf or hard of hearing is not a visible impairment. It's not as obvious as some disabilities are.

Even though progress may be slow for the hearing impaired, it doesn't mean that amazing breakthroughs can't happen. In May 2011, Sloan was in the car driving and heard a radio ad for a device called the Esteem Hearing Implant. The ad stated that it was fully implantable and used all the natural components of the ear to provide natural hearing versus mechanical hearing (like you get with a hearing aid or a cochlear device). He told me about it and told me to get on the computer, find the website, and research the implant. Sloan just

knew that this was the device for me—the device that
I'd had been told years ago was "coming down the pipes
in about ten years' time."

I sat down at the computer and feverishly began
to research all I could. (I have to admit that I'm still not
well-versed with all of the mechanics and terminology
for the Esteem device. All I cared about was whether
it worked or not and if it did indeed give you natural
hearing, as the company stated. Sloan is the one who
knows the ins and outs of the device, the history behind
it, its funding, and how it actually works. I usually just
let him explain every time someone asks questions that
leave me grabbing for words.) I found Envoy Medical's
website with ease and was able to fill out a questionnaire
to request information to be mailed to me. Upon further
digging, I was able to get a contact number to call for
more information.

Now, I always had a hatred for calling any type
of customer service or any kind of office or basically

anyone who didn't know me well. To make the process a *little* smoother, I had always owned cell phones that were "hearing aid compatible" and had extremely loud volume levels. I had perfected the art of holding said cell phone in a precise spot over my hearing aid speaker. I'd usually announce that I was a hearing aid user and would need them to speak loudly and clearly and that they may have to repeat themselves. During a call, if there was a slight accent or if they spoke quietly, mumbled, or held the phone funny, I didn't stand a chance of being able to interact.

When you are wearing hearing aids because of a severe hearing impairment, a phone call is a very different experience than it is for someone with a "normal" hearing ability. During the occasional times that I would talk to someone on the phone, I learned that certain questions only have a few choices for an answer. Over the years, I learned to distinguish the way a "yes" or a "no" sounded and other common responses. If I got stumped, I simply reworded the question and asked them again. Sometimes, I would say things like "Okay, so it will be $9.99 for the bowl?" and the person on the other end of the line would either say "yes" or "no" and we would go from there. I learned to cope and finagle questions to make it work, and if I was stumped, I told them I'd call back later or I'd get Sloan or someone else on the phone.

Even with all that, I usually made Sloan make any phone calls that required a lot of effort; or if I attempted such a call, I'd get a few words into it and just hand him the phone, to which he'd say, "I'm sorry, ma'am/sir, but my wife is deaf and wears hearing aids; could you please talk to me instead?"

However, with my newfound discovery of the Esteem, I didn't hesitate. I called and was greeted right away by a lady who spoke clearly and loudly. Their website stated that they had this kind of customer service, and they meant it! Not only that, but the lady I was speaking to informed me that her husband was actually deaf and that she was quite accustomed to repeating things and speaking in a way that could be understood. I began to ask her questions at machine-gun speed. After I explained my hearing loss and answered her questions, we began to discuss whether insurance companies would pay for the device. She informed me that because the device was so new to the market and was just FDA approved, it was not, in fact, covered. I then asked her how much the device cost. She paused for a moment and then told me it was $30,000. My heart jumped into my throat, and I gasped. $30,000? I was crushed. She may as well have said it was $30 million.

I promptly ended my conversation and called Sloan to let him know all I had found out. When I told him the cost of the device, he didn't miss a beat. He was quick to be positive and say, "Don't worry about the cost; call the lady back and find out what you need to do to get the ball rolling and see if you are, in fact, a candidate."

So I did. I called her back, and after mentioning to her that $30,000 was a lot of money, she told me that it was actually $30,000 PER EAR. I began to sob on the phone with this complete stranger and tell her how that just wasn't achievable and that I was sorry I wasted her time. I really don't remember everything I said, but I know that I was on the phone for several minutes just sobbing and rambling on and on to her.

I finally hung up and called Sloan back and relayed the info to him while sobbing some more. I'll never forget what he said: "Do not worry about the cost. I will sell a kidney, I will join the army, and I will sell our house. I will do whatever it takes to make this happen." He was not kidding, and I knew this, only adding to my anxiety. We began to talk, and he had to remind me that we serve an awesome God who has provided for us in dire times and that God would continue to provide and make a way when chances seemed slim. He just kept telling me, "If this is meant to happen, it will. God will provide."

During this phone call, I was reminded of our time in China. I had been having a hard time with my hearing, and my hearing aids weren't working. I was really discouraged, and my father in-law Ross told me to remember a certain scripture in Hebrews: "He who promised IS faithful." I clung to that passage desperately at times when I was frustrated with my ears. During the talk with Sloan, I started to feel like this device was part of God's plan for me, but I was having a hard time wrapping my mind around the fact that it would cost $60,000.

For several days, I was depressed and moped about. I'd cry randomly when I'd remember that there was a "cure" for my deafness out there, but it was just beyond my reach. It was during this time that family and friends as well as people I didn't even know began to chip in and donate money to me. I think we received a little over $5,000 from these kind people in just a matter of days. It was humbling to know that so many

cared and that dear friends and family who didn't
have a lot of money were still handing us checks for
amounts as small as $25 just because they wanted to
support us and be a part of what they felt would be
my miracle.

Before long, my mother-in-law, Lari, came to
us and said that she felt led to help. She said she had
prayed about it and just really felt like the Lord was
asking her to provide. She had only enough money
to cover the cost for one ear, but she said she had
complete peace about it. I was completely and utterly
overwhelmed. My newly widowed mother-in-law was
willing to cash out her retirement savings so that I
could get a hearing implant. In my mind, it was $30,000
that could sustain her for quite some time in the event
something happened and she had to quit work or had
some kind of emergency. She was willing to just cash it
out and, without hesitation and fully trusting in God,
give it to me.

There are no words to describe the emotions I felt. I was incredibly moved that she was so willing to give— and give wholeheartedly. I knew Lari very well and knew she wouldn't make such a gesture without giving it much prayer and thought. I knew she was 100% sure and wouldn't be swayed. So I accepted her generous gift with deep gratitude.

Soon, the process began. I learned that I needed to get an MRI to make sure the bone structure in my ear was fit for surgery. I did that and also sent in an audiogram for the doctor to look over. Once that was done and I was cleared as an official candidate, I received my surgery date of August 24, 2011.

Later on, after my surgery was complete and my implant was activated, my mother-in-law took a few days to get away. She went to visit a dear friend of hers in Nashville, Tennessee. I remember she said she just needed a getaway, some time to just enjoy herself and not have any stress or sorrows on her mind. She had a great time and was able to relax and recharge.

On her flight home, she witnessed a massive thunderstorm. She had a window seat, and she described to us what it was like to be riding through the clouds amidst rain, thunder, and lightning. She said part of her was terrified, but another part of her was just enamored by the beauty and strength of the storm and being right in the middle of it as it took place. She described the lightning striking right outside her window as "absolutely magnificent." She said that she was having quiet time and talking with God and praying. She said that she began to reflect on what a rough time she'd had lately with her husband's passing and other troubles. She said she told God, "You know, if you were to ask me right now what I'd like, I'd like for something magnificent to happen. We just really need something *magnificent* in our lives right now."

She went on to tell us how she just poured her heart out to God and repeated her wish, "You didn't do it for me when Ross died, and you didn't do it for me during other hard times in my life. No matter what, I have always and will always continue to love and serve you all the days of my life. But just in case, if you wanted to know what I'd like right now, I'd like for us to experience something magnificent." As we would all soon discover, God was listening.

So, back to the week of my surgery, we drove the three-and-a-half hours down to The Woodlands near Houston, Texas, where Envoy Medical had a surgery center. The day before surgery, I had a pre-op visit to go over my medical history once more, to answer any questions I had, and to check my vitals and so forth. Early on the morning of surgery, after kissing Sloan bye, I was wheeled away toward the operating room with a hopeful heart.

Surgery lasted a little over nine hours, which isn't typical; but because of the makeup of the bones in my ear and the fact that I have a very small ear cavity, my surgery took more time than most. They made two incisions. One incision was directly behind the ear, where they ran two wires down to the ear canal and attached a driver and a sensor to two different bones. The other incision was in the skull, where they ground away a portion of the skull and implanted the processor. [With this type of device, once implanted and turned on, the processor picks up sound and causes the driver and sensor to vibrate, which then sends sound waves to the brain.]

When my surgery was complete, I remember waking up, seeing Sloan, and immediately starting to cry and holler. I kept telling him about my father-in-law Ross, as well as Jesus, being by my bedside the entire time I was out. In my medicated state, I kept telling Sloan that Jesus sat down the whole time and would never look at me. He wore a white robe and simply sat with His hands in His lap. There was complete peace during the whole experience, but Sloan said I kept asking him, "Why did Jesus sit? Why wouldn't He stand up and look at me?" and then telling him, "Don't let me forget they were there; I want to remember every detail!"

The thing that stood out most to me was the fact that Ross, my father-in-law, was actually the one who stood by my bedside the entire time. He was wearing his typical red plaid button-down shirt and had his pinky fingers hooked into his belt loops the way he always had in life when he was just standing around chatting. This sight, too, was very comforting and gave me a sense of peace. I realize that I was under anesthesia and skating along the brink of death, unconscious for nine plus hours; but 'til the day I die, I will remember that.

There were other things that were very unpleasant upon waking up, like feeling that I was floating and the room was spinning. I didn't realize that being under anesthesia that long was so hard on a person's body and that coming back is not fun. I was able to return home the next day after my post-op visit, but it was ten days before I felt normal again. However, I should note that much like childbirth, within weeks, I was willing to do the surgery all over again.

Every mother knows what I mean. Those hours may have been the worst pain you've ever endured and the most energy you've ever had to exert toward something, but within a few weeks, you forget about the pain and hardship because you've gotten something much greater out of it. A mother gets a baby, a tiny new life that will profoundly affect and change her, and bring her joy in so many ways. Getting a new ear and experiencing what it could do for me made me quickly forget the blood, sweat, and tears. I was ready for round two!

Incidentally, one of the only frustrating aspects to the device is that you have to wait eight weeks after surgery for activation. You don't get to have it turned on right away because they want eight weeks of healing time—time for all the fluids to drain and the swelling to go down. I won't lie: that was the longest eight weeks of my life! I did okay for the first few weeks, but the last three were really hard. I had to strain with one ear, and I was feeling completely unbalanced and disoriented. I was easily worn out and mentally exhausted, and I felt so off balance and out of sorts. I was having a hard time picking up on vibrations and focusing. Imagine having to wear a patch over one of your eyes for eight weeks and not being able to take the patch off. It gets old fast.

The last week of September arrived, and originally we were all going to load up and head down to the medical center. But at the last minute, my mother-in-law decided that she'd stay here with our girls, and Sloan and I would go alone. After some consideration, we decided that it would be better to have as much quiet as possible on my ride home with my ear turned on. I figured it was going to be overwhelming enough, and

Lari suggested that I'd probably not be able to handle our two active, chatty little girls in the back seat the whole three-and-half-hour car ride home.

The day we left, Lari handed Sloan her camera, literally as we were loading up into the car and said, "Here, take my camera and film Sarah's reaction as they turn the device on." Sloan absolutely hates taking pictures or being in charge of a camera, but he grudgingly took it. He'll be the first to tell you that had it not been his mother asking and had she not paid for the device, he would not have taken the camera.

The whole ride down, I was nervous. I kept thinking things like "What if it doesn't work?" or "What if I don't like it?" This was twenty-nine years in the making, and I was beside myself with all sorts of emotions. I was just as excited as I was terrified. As much as I longed and desired for this opportunity, I was scared. As crazy as it sounds, there was a certain sense of comfort being the way I was. I woke up every day knowing how it would be, knowing that I'd be reading lips and working hard to fit in. It was a routine I had perfected it, and it was comfortable. I was nervous about this new thing I was about to experience. I knew it was going to be the biggest change I had experienced thus far in my life and would force me to grow as a person in ways I couldn't imagine.

We arrived at the center, and after the typical routine and questions, the moment came when I was seated in the chair and Melinda the technician was doing some testing on the device to make sure everything was okay. She ran her full gamut of tests and did some things on the computer with her program, and then she told me, "Okay, we're ready; are you?" I held the remote for the device up to my ear. My hand was shaking so badly that it actually took three tries because the remote has to be held over the device a certain way in order for it to work. Melinda hit a button, and for the first time in my life, I heard something clearly ...

Eight

Sitting there in that chair, my mind was running a million miles a minute. A big part of me was absolutely terrified that, for some odd reason, I'd be the first person that this device didn't work for. I have always stated that I believe that nothing in life is 100% guaranteed; so even though there was no reason for it to malfunction, I was worried. I was also terrified that I would hate the way it sounded. I had a certain sense of comfort with my daily life—knowing what to expect. My fear of the unknown— even though the unknown was what I had dreamed about since I was a child—was very real. As I've mentioned, in the years I had worn hearing aids, every time I got a new pair, I hated them. I hated the adjustment, and I missed the familiarity of the old pair every time. So here I was, nervous that they'd turn it on, I'd hate it, and then I'd feel awful about the fact that my widowed mother-in-law had cashed out her savings for this device. Another huge part of me was incredibly excited and curious. I was dying to know what it was like to have "normal" ears. I wanted to experience all the things I had missed out on. I wanted to be able to function in society normally and without the stress, fear, embarrassment, and anxiety that came with having hearing loss. I was dying to know what it was like to hear clearly.

And so it was a beep—the nicest, loudest, clearest beep ever! And it signaled a new life and opened a wellspring of emotions in me that had been building up for twenty-nine years. Then I heard the remote being set down on the counter, and I was absolutely amazed and relieved all at the same time. It's hard for me to explain; but in those brief moments during the process of activation, I experienced a complete sense of clarity. In the seconds before it happened, I knew the device was on, and I knew the moment a noise was made, I'd hear it. To me, it was an absolute miracle. In that moment, I experienced what I had waited for all my life. Melinda began speaking, and I was hearing her! Part of me was immediately relieved that it worked and that Lari's money had been well spent. The other part of me was so excited because I liked it. I liked hearing! Right away, I could tell that hearing was a good thing and that I would not regret the surgery and all the tears shed over the last few weeks. As these thoughts and emotions were running through my mind, I heard Melinda say, "How does it sound?"

I started to answer her, and I realized I could hear the noises coming from my mouth. Then I realized how I sounded, and I got choked up. Then I laughed, and that sent me into a fit of tears. All these sounds were intensified because I was hearing all this from inside myself for the first time, and I was completely and utterly overwhelmed like you cannot imagine. I feared my heart was gonna explode, and I just couldn't put into words what was racing through my mind. I started thinking, "I don't want to hear myself cry; this is weird," which I said out loud and which made me giggle even more.

I was a huge mess, but I was a good mess.

The doctors and specialists continued to run their testing and mapping program to tweak the device to suit my needs, all while I sat there, still in amazement and grinning from ear to ear. Sloan only shot ninety-one seconds of video, simply so his mother could see the moment of activation and my response. After he put the camera down, they told him to ask me a question. He covered his mouth with his hand, and he said,

"Do you want a cucumber sandwich?"

Twelve years I've been with this man, ten years I've been married to him, two children I've given him, and that's what he choose to say to me for the first time I got to hear him with a good ear? That didn't matter to me in that moment; it was the sweetest thing I had ever heard. I repeated his sentence back, to which the whole room cracked up laughing. One person said, "What the heck? Why'd you say that?" Sloan's defense was that he didn't want to say something cliché, and he knew me well enough to know that even if he covered his mouth, I would recognize his facial expression and muscles saying the words "I love you" or something common like that. Plus, those who know Sloan like I do will understand that I wouldn't have expected anything less from him than a silly comment to make me smile and make the moment memorable.

Once we were finished, we hopped in our car to head home. I immediately grabbed Sloan's phone and called his mom because I wanted to talk to my girls. Lari answered and was asking me how it was, did I like it, and was it all I hoped it to be. I heard my girls in the background, and I got choked up. Olivia got on the phone and said, "Hi, Mommy. I love you." I told her I loved her back, and then I lost it. I started bawling and gasping for air, and I couldn't catch my breath. I handed Sloan the phone so he could finish the conversation.

Not far down the road and a few minutes after I caught my breath, we pulled in to an Outback Steakhouse to have dinner with Sloan's cousin, who lived in the area. I stepped out of the car and was taken aback by how noisy the nearby highway was. I could hear cars honking and engines revving, and it was incredible! We sat down at our table, and I kept saying how loud the restaurant was. The waitress came over and took our order, and I was floored that I was able to order and answer her questions without having to look at Sloan and wait for him to help me out. I sat there more than likely looking like an idiot and grinning at every noise I was experiencing.

The waitress brought our drinks, and I was jumping out of my skin because, to me, it sounded as though

she was slamming the cups down onto the table. Sloan
assured me that everything I was hearing at this point
was normal. Our food arrived. I took one bite of my
salad, and I panicked. It was so *loud*! The chewing, the
crunching, the swallowing—it was so overwhelming
to me. At this point, I became concerned because
I discovered that I couldn't chew and hear someone talk
at the same time. I had to stop chewing to listen, and
when someone started eating, I'd hurry up and eat so
I could be done by the time they started talking again.
I was questioning Sloan about if this was normal, as I
couldn't imagine having to spend my life knowing that
so many conversations would happen at a dinner table
that I might miss hearing. He quickly reminded me that
the doctors had warned me that my brain was firing
in ways it had never fired before and that I'd adjust;
distractions like eating would become background noise,
and I wouldn't always notice it or be unable to eat and
listen to a conversation at the same time.

Powered On

We finished up eating and got back into our car.
The whole ride home, I was enamored with so many
sounds and already overwhelmed at the noisy world
around me. The road noise was incredibly loud and
shocking to me. I couldn't understand how folks had
conversations in the car with the engine revving, the
brakes, the tires, and other cars honking. It was crazy.
Sloan asked me if I wanted some music, and of course,
I did.

Right before turning on the radio, I was anxious.
I knew so many people who had such a love for music.
I had always wanted to experience it fully for myself,
and I was so looking forward to the moment in which I
would finally hear it the way it was meant to be heard.
We turned on the radio, and I started flipping through
channels. Right away, Sloan was giggling because I had
the volume MUCH lower than I normally did, and if he
put it where he liked it, I thought it was extremely loud.

I have to admit that the whole ride home, I was
sad. Music did not sound good at all to me. I was half
panicked and didn't mention it to Sloan right away.
Music was a big part of what I wanted to experience,
and I thought it would be so great right away. I
confessed my worries shortly before we got home, and
Sloan quickly reminded me that listening would take
some practice and getting used to. I later found out that
I'd need adjustments to tweak the device and to make
everything sound the way it should. Until I had my first
adjustment, music wasn't what I imagined it would be.

We got home pretty late that night, and I was
exhausted, but running on adrenaline fumes. We
climbed into bed after I posted my video online so my
friends and family could see my activation. I laid there
in the dark and, for the first time in my life, whispered
with my husband. We held hands and discussed life and
this new blessing I was getting to experience. It was

completely surreal to me, and I never want to forget that feeling.

Sloan drifted off to sleep, but my mind would not shut down, and I was still awake. I had decided that I wanted to leave the implant on so I could experience what "normal" people do at night. But the second Sloan started snoring like a bulldog, I changed my mind. I tried to deal with it at first, but between his snoring and every little bitty noise my old farm house made, I was getting frazzled. "Normal" could wait until morning. I turned my ear off and passed out in my comfortable cocoon of silence.

The next morning, I woke up anxious to turn on my ear and see my girls. Sloan had gotten them out of bed, and I hurried into the kitchen where he brought them to play. They saw me, started asking me questions and telling me they loved me, and then promptly went back to the tea party they were having. They were three and one; they didn't fully grasp that my world was turned upside down overnight. Sloan left the room, and I sat down on the floor and just took it all in. I watched them play and talk to each other, and I really paid attention to their role-play and their voices and tones. The faces they made as they spoke were darling.

Before I knew it, I was crying and quietly sobbing so as not to disturb them. I wanted to sit on that floor in the sunlight and watch them, in their innocence, play forever. In that moment, every dollar spent, every tear shed, and every pain I had experienced in the weeks and months prior was worth it. Sloan came back into the room, and when he spotted me, he ran over and started asking me what was wrong. "Are you okay?" he asked. I choked out that I was fine, but had the girls always sounded like this? Are they always this animated, or are they extra wound up this morning? He looked so moved as he realized my concern and told me that they were their normal selves. At about this time, the girls noticed Sloan and I on the floor and began to ask me what was wrong, saying, "You ok Momma?" My heart was completely overfilled with love and appreciation for this moment, for this chance.

I later began to realize how I would have felt if I had waited until the girls were ten and twelve. I couldn't imagine missing out on all the things I have gotten to experience as they have grown up. I believe being a mother is the highest calling a woman can experience in her lifetime. After hearing my girls' tiny laughs, I knew I had made the right decision in going forward with the hearing implant. I have no regrets.

I should point out that I don't mean that deaf mothers can't enjoy motherhood with every ounce of their being. When I was deaf, I experienced it all in ways hearing mothers may not understand. I studied body language and mannerisms and focused intensely on my girls. Because I couldn't enjoy their voices, the noises they made, or the tone with which they said things, I learned to fully appreciate their facial expressions and their physical interactions. Being a good mother has nothing to do with whether you can hear your children well; it's about loving them and teaching them all that you know. I have been blessed with two wonderful little girls who teach me about life every day. I'm glad I've been able to experience it from both sides of the hearing spectrum.

In the coming days, I experienced millions of new sounds—birds chirping in the trees, leaves rustling along the ground, our horses running through the pasture, cows mooing, dogs barking, raindrops, gunshots, my bulldogs grunting and snorting, the air conditioner running, the fridge, the microwave, my loud diesel truck, the water trickling down and pitter-pattering as I showered, water running in the sink, my fish tank pump running, all my internal noises, the cicadas outside at night along with the bullfrogs, knocks on doors, my own footsteps, people breathing, my kids smacking, zippers. The list goes on and on and on. Even still, to this day, the list continues to grow. At least once a week, I tell Sloan my truck is running funny, and it never is. Several times a day, I run outside or upstairs thinking something is wrong with the girls, only to find them playing. I still jump when a phone rings or the AC comes on. Public toilets are insanely loud and make my heart pound every time I flush one. Loud restaurants or bars wear me out, and I find myself getting tired at parties or gatherings very easily. Over time, it has gotten better, and it will continue to get better as I continue to acclimate.

I'm twenty-nine years old, and I'm experiencing life for the first time again. I enjoyed life in my own way before, but now I get to experience it much differently. I've seen both sides of a disability, and I'm forever changed by it.

Nine

Many along the way have asked why I've had this surgery. Some think I should not have interfered with "how God made me;" some think I should have embraced being deaf. From the first time I can remember, I've always done the best I could with what I had, but I always desired to be made whole—as I saw it. I make no apologies about what I want in my life. There was never a point where I just gave in and didn't long for good, working ears. Looking back now, I can see that God provided me with the tools and the personality to endure and do well—to make the most of my life until He was ready for me to experience hearing. I honestly believe that we all have a testimony that can be used to help others. My testimony is about being positive and having faith that waiting decades for something can be worthwhile.

Looking back over the last year of my life, remembering all those who have contacted me through e-mails and the ones who have spoken to me on the street, I can see how I've affected people. As hard as it is for me to say that, and as odd as it sounds to me, I've come to realize that my life, my story, has helped people. That is such a humbling thing to experience. I love and serve a God who proves His faithfulness time and time again in ways I'm continually amazed by. When I ask God for something, I don't give him a timeline. That's taken a long time for me to learn, but I've learned that through His timing, all things work together for the greater good. I look back at the life I've lived and think to myself, everything *was* worth the wait.

Other than the obvious desire to hear, what was it I waited for? Better self-esteem, the chance for independence, the ability to feel more engaged as a mother, as a wife, and as a friend. Since being activated, my self-esteem has soared. I no longer worry non-stop about how others perceive me. I don't worry about missing out on what is being said. I can interact in society with confidence. I can now go out and not worry about needing someone to constantly help me or keep me filled in. The game of appearing to know what's going on is no longer necessary. My smile is always a genuine smile now and never one that says that I hope they don't think I'm dumb or rude. I can now interact with my kids at any level and not just one-on-one and face-to-face. We can run and play outside, and I can still be in tune with them and not miss out on a single thing they say. They don't have to work so hard to get my attention or to focus on me. Instead of being woken up in the morning with a little hand shoving a hearing aid in my face, my girls can climb up into my bed and ask for cartoons and breakfast. Sloan and I can now lie in bed at night with the lights off and discuss our life and what we are grateful for. All of these things, all the noises that bring joy to my heart, and so much more are the reasons I chose to get a hearing implant.

I look back and cannot imagine passing this opportunity up. I think I have always felt like a hearing person born in a deaf person's body. It never felt right, and I never accepted it. It always felt like something was missing. I just always held on to hope that one day I'd be able to function well in the world, feel whole, and find what made me complete.

That being said, I started realizing that there were others out there like me—people who longed to feel whole and wanted to experience the things I had. These people are the ones who tug at my heartstrings daily. In the U.S. alone, there are thirty-six million people with a hearing disability at the last count—*thirty-six million people in the US alone.* If even a small percentage of those feel the way I do and could benefit from a hearing implant, they should be able to get one.

When I got my own implant, I didn't imagine that fate would put me in a position to help create awareness on behalf of those people in a very public way. Two days after Sloan uploaded my activation video to YouTube for our friends and family to see, the CEO of Envoy Medical called. He explained that the video had gone viral and that *The Today Show* was trying to reach me. I was absolutely dumbfounded. I threw the kids into the truck and rushed down to the barn where Sloan was. I had to ask him what "going viral" meant exactly. In those first two days, the video had been viewed by over 250,000 people. After seventy-two hours, that number surpassed a million.

The next thing I knew, I was booked to appear live in New York on *The Today Show,* and the whirlwind began. When word got out in my town, people started calling and offering me clothes to wear on TV; hair salons were offering to do my hair. People were sharing in my excitement and blessing me left and right. I was overwhelmed.

Sloan and I flew to New York, and I was interviewed for *The Today Show*. While there, we were contacted by the producers of *The Ellen DeGeneres Show,* among other shows. I was invited to appear on those programs as well. We flew home for twelve hours to grab our girls, re-pack, and fly back out.

Appearing on *Ellen* will forever be etched in my memory as one of the highlights of my life. When I'm old and on my deathbed, I will remember that day. It was October 4th, the day before my twenty-ninth birthday. The producers had flown us there, and at the last moment, they'd asked if Lari could come with us. We were so excited to meet Ellen DeGeneres and to be a part of her show. During the pre-interview process, one of the questions asked was, "Is there anyone you'd like to thank while you're on the show?" I stated that yes, indeed, I wanted to thank my mother-in-law. I explained how she had cashed out her retirement savings to pay for the surgery, that she was newly widowed, and that we loved her and thought the world of her. They then told me, "Well, then we'll be sure to give you some 'swag' to thank her with."

Needless to say, the whole time we were getting ready to appear on the show, I was so excited to see what they would bless Lari with. I was hoping for a new wardrobe or a trip to some exotic spa or a new purse. I had no idea what they were planning.

I'll never forget sitting on the stage and being mesmerized by Ellen's charisma and gorgeous smile. I was so nervous about meeting her and being on the show in front of a live audience. She began the interview, we chatted (she is *hysterical* by the way), and then she said, "Well, we think a family shouldn't have to struggle like this. So NOT ONLY IS ENVOY GOING

TO DO HER OTHER EAR FOR FREE … but …"
and then she whipped out a huge plastic check that
had been hidden next to her chair. It was a check for
$30,000 so that we could pay Lari back for her generous
gift! I was so overcome with emotion; I couldn't focus.
She had my family come up on stage with me, and the
look on Lari's face was priceless! I whispered in her
ear, "I thought you'd get a day at the spa!" Ha! We were
all just shocked. We hugged Ellen and thanked her
for the awesome surprise. I really wished I'd had the
opportunity to talk with her longer or hang out back
stage with her. She was a really cool person and had such
an aura about her. Her happiness was infectious.

We headed home later that day, and you can bet
we carted that huge plastic check home with us. Just
picture me shuffling through the airport, trying to keep
the check modestly hidden and then boarding the plane
and trying to find a place for it. A group of guys on a
"bachelor weekend" found me an empty baggage cabinet

to squeeze my check into. Of course, they wanted to know what it was for, and all I could do was blush furiously and say, "It's a long story, guys."

Upon returning from the *Ellen* appearance, we thought the madness was over. We never imagined it was only the beginning of our journey, and we never anticipated our phones would continue to ring and people would continue to request interviews. Believe it or not, we are quiet, private people for the most part. We have our small circle of friends, and we enjoy our life outside of city limits and away from the bright lights.

Sloan and I sat down one night and discussed the opportunities at hand. We realized we were at a point that we needed to decide to either stop talking to people or else use the opportunity to achieve a greater goal, that goal being to help convince insurance companies to start covering the implant. The thirty-six million hearing disabled folks in the U.S. deserved to have this option.

Powered On

After my talk with Sloan, I moved forward with this purpose in mind. I made a commitment of sorts, one in which I wasn't going turn down any publicity if it continued to get the word out about the Esteem Implant and if it might get the attention of insurance companies and those who make policy. I started mentioning it in every interview from that point on. Whether I helped to get things rolling or if they coincidently started snowballing shortly thereafter, I don't know, but progress has been made! Blue Cross Blue Shield started covering the device in a few states, with some other insurance companies currently following suit. AT&T covers it for their employees and pays for everything door to door, minus a rental car. The VA started covering it for the brave men and women who have served this country. I have also been told of a few small, private companies that now cover it as well.

What took fifteen years for the Cochlear to achieve, the Esteem has accomplished in a matter of months. I can only hope that the momentum continues and that more and more people are able to start receiving the device. There is nothing worse than realizing something is just within your grasp, but you can't have it. I want everyone who desires it to be able to have the same life-changing opportunity I've had.

Ten

From the day my activation video went viral, life has been a crazy whirlwind for me. I still find myself waking up in the morning and going, "Wow! That really happened!" I jokingly tell Sloan that this is how God will keep me humble: I'll continue to wake up daily in amazement. All joking aside, I don't feel as if anything in my life has changed other than my ears. However, at least a few times a week, someone will say, "Hey, superstar!" or "You're famous!" I never know how to take it or how to act. It makes me uncomfortable because while I want to express to these people my gratitude,

I don't feel any more special than I did five years ago. I just feel blessed. I feel blessed to have been able to travel so much and meet so many inspiring people all over. I feel blessed to be able to share my story.

Every single time I return from a television interview, I spend the whole hour-ride home from the airport in a state of disbelief that I've just flown somewhere to talk with a famous person. I still think, "They wanted to talk to *me*?!? Did I really just go on TV?!?" Then Sloan and I return home, and life goes on normally for us. We still have trucks that break down, my kids are still covered in mud and riding horses half-naked, I still love grooming dogs so I can have money to spend at the thrift store, and on some days, I forget to brush my teeth. Then randomly the phone will ring, and I'm once again shocked that someone wants to talk to me.

Basically, I live my life doing what I love and spending time with those I love. I don't focus on tomorrow. My identity is only in trying to be a good person and helping everyone I can as long as I breathe. I want to make a mark in the world. I want to know that when I die, someone somewhere was changed because of me. If we could all change one person in the course of our lives, that act would affect all of us. I care nothing about the corporate world; I care nothing about becoming famous; I care nothing about anything other than just living life as life comes at me. I strive daily to be a better person than I was yesterday. We all can better ourselves daily. I encourage folks to break out of their box. Step outside yourself and examine your life and those in it. Help when you can; give when you have it; listen to God and put Him first in all you do. Love with your whole heart. Treat people—*all* people—with respect. Take into consideration that you never know what people are going through or what they have gone through. Hold doors open, use your manners, and always smile. Life can be hard; it can bring you to what you think is the end of your rope. I realize it's hard to stay positive all the time; we all struggle with it. However, I also realize we make the choice of what our outlook is. We wake up each day determining our attitude. If only it was as easy as pushing a button every morning! It's not, and that fight—that decision to turn lemons into lemonade daily—is what builds our character and adds to the timeline that is our life.

As I've mentioned, so many times I hear, "God will not give you more than you can handle." You know what? How dare we think we are above a little challenge, above a little heartache, blood, sweat and tears? God sometimes gives us more than we THINK we can handle, but what so many fail to see or realize is that He also provides us with the tools and the ability to overcome those obstacles.

You see, even when you can't hear, you are on your last dime, your dogs died, your tractor and truck are broken down, your welder was stolen, your father-in-law, uncle, and grandpa died, you scraped your knee, you lost

a baby, you lost a job, you lost friends, your house was

broken into, you lost your phone, your glasses were bent,

your pastures were brown and dried up, your horse was

crippled, you lost livestock, your roof got a leak, you got

a ticket, your well stopped working, you lost a debit card,

and your heel broke on your shoe—even with all that—

someone somewhere can learn a lesson from you.

If you are really open, you can still find joy in

anything. If you woke up breathing today, there is still

something to be grateful and happy for—your children's

smiles, your spouse's loving embrace, the sunshine, the

wind in your face, a rainbow, an unexpected check in

the mail, warm chocolate chip cookies that turn out just

right, flowers blooming, the perfect garage sale, money

in a pocket, being taken out to dinner, kind words from

a stranger, free movie tickets, winning a pair of boots,

making a new friend, raindrops on your face, dancing

around the house with the windows up on a perfect

Powered On

Spring day, new life being born, reading a good book, the perfect bubble bath, the wind rustling through the trees, the rooster crowing in your yard, the laughter of children, your favorite song being played on the radio, having a faithful mother-in-law, receiving two new ears, and the ability to finally be *Powered On*.

Facing Page: Video screen shots from the actual moment of getting **Powered On**. To watch the video, search for Sarah Churman on YouTube or use the following link: http://www.youtube.com/watch?v=LsOo3jzkhYA

Special Thanks to:

Adam Tillinghast for your endurance in all the "rabbit trails" we've journeyed together and for having a heart like His.

My mother-in-law, Lari, for being a prime example of a Godly woman and for being faithful and having a heart to listen. Thank you for always loving me as your own. This book wouldn't be possible without your generosity.

Photo Courtesy of Misty Adams

Father-in-law, Ross

Mother-in-law, Lari

My parents, Michael and Judy, for giving me unconditional love, for always making my childhood fun and giving me many happy memories. Dad, you always told me, "The smartest man in the world wouldn't be smart unless he read books." Well, after reading so many books, I got to write one! Mom, you always told me to "Be myself and not worry what anyone else thought." That has served me so well in life. I love you both so much.

My husband, Sloan. Thank you for always being my rock. Thank you for always having my back and giving me your all. Thank you for loving me and treating me like I'm the only woman in your world and propelling me, affirming me, and building me up daily. I pray our girls find a man half as good as you.

1 Corinthians 13:4–8a
Love is patient, love is kind. It does not envy, it does not boast, it is not proud. It is not rude, it is not self-seeking, it is not easily angered, it keeps no record of wrongs. Love does not delight in evil but rejoices with the truth. It always protects, always trusts, always hopes, always perseveres. Love never fails …

Thank you for never failing me. I love you "to the moon and back."

—Sarah.

Photo Courtesy of Luis Pena

Thank you to all my family and friends. I unfortunately cannot fill up pages and pages explaining what you all mean to me. Please know that I love you all, and I appreciate all of your support and standing by my side from the moment of surgery until now.

Last but certainly not least, thank you to all those who along my journey have sent well wishes, prayers, and words of encouragement. My Facebook, YouTube, and e-mail accounts have been overflowing  with messages from folks all around the world. You guys, the ones who see me through a screen, are the ones this book is for—the ones who need a "pick me up" when life gets rough. I pray this book speaks to you, or if nothing else, at least brightens your day.

Photo Courtesy of Misty Adams

Powered On

Photo Courtesy of Whitnae Churman

Photo Courtesy of Luis Pena

Acknowledgments

I would like to acknowledge these folks who contributed time, goods, or services along the way that helped create this book, make my appearances possible, etc.

In no particular order:

Envoy Medical. I'm forever grateful for the man who had a dream 30 plus years ago and sat down at his kitchen table and drew up the implant I now use. I'm grateful for the hearts of those at this company who saw it fit to bless me with the free implant and the money to pay Lari back for cashing out her savings.

Ellen DeGeneres and her producers. Without your interest in my story, my life may not be on the path it is today. Without your kind spirit to give, my mother-in-law would not have any savings. I'm forever grateful to you for your efforts in contacting Envoy and the lifelong impact it made.

Photo Courtesy of The Ellen DeGeneres Show

R&B Marketing's Rebecca Brian. Thank you for putting together my first book signing. I'm blessed to call you my friend.

Jeremy Farrar. Thank you for painting a portrait of me getting my device turned on. You singlehandedly captured a moment that will forever be etched in my mind and is now displayed in my home.

Teri Collazo. You kindly provided me with clothes to wear on my very first interviews including *The Today Show.* Without you, I'd still be digging in my closet frantically.

Aspirations and Delilah McMasters. Thank you for your generous donation toward funding more clothes for other interviews so that I'm once again not left frantically digging through my closet. You ladies truly understand the importance of a great outfit.

The gals at The Ritz Salon and Spa and Krista Bingham. You guys freed up a spot in your schedules at the last minute to do my hair for *The Today Show.* I'll forever be grateful to you for that. Not only that, you went above and beyond and blessed me with a shirt and some jewelry to walk around NY in style.

My "Computer Man" who at his request will remain nameless. Thank you for blessing me with a laptop so this book could be written. Without your kind gift at just the perfect time, I would be lost.

Photos Courtesy of Kelli Ahern

Josh Weathers. I'll never forget being down at the barn after learning that my video went viral. You said, "Just wait, Ellen will contact you." I thought you were nuts. Turns out, not only can you play the most amazing music, but you're psychic! Thank you for playing at my first book signing. I hope with all my heart that "your time" is coming. You and your family deserve all the world has to offer you!

To the photographers who allowed me to use their photographs in this book: Luis Peña, Misty Adams, Kelli Ahern, Rick Gilbert and Whitnae Churman. You guys all have a gift and a way with the camera. Thanks for capturing such moments in our lives. Misty, thank you for being such an amazing friend!

Cheryl Leb & Kelly, Hart & Hallman. Thank you for graciously agreeing to see me at the beginning of this book deal to go over the contract and help us understand all the legal jargon. You are kind, sincere, and had a heart to help. Without you, the contract may not have gotten signed.

To anyone else I may have forgotten (and I sincerely hope that's no one), thank you so much for all you have done to make this journey possible.

Special Gift for Readers

Josh Weathers is a prime example of the American musician; he plays music because he *loves* music. He and his band, The Josh Weathers Band, started at the bottom playing anywhere they could and now have a fan base that supports 6,000 patrons to a Tuesday night concert—in a parking lot! He is included in this section because he invited Sarah to one of his concerts after her first implant was activated. It was the first concert she could really "hear"—and mind you, it was still only out of one ear. Needless to say, she was enamored and has been an avid concert fan since. That night opened the door to her pursing the enjoyment of music; and for the first time, she understood what she had been missing all these years. Josh Weathers is included in this "thank you" section for his kindness as well as to give you, the reader, a sense of what music Sarah enjoys. Josh has generously given all of you some free music as well. Simply go to link below and follow the instructions for your *Powered On* free music download. We hope you enjoy this small gift; it is something personal Sarah and I felt we could give to each person who has purchased this book aside from our heartfelt thank you.

Photo Courtesy of RMcQueenPhoto.com

Go to: www.joshweathersband.com/poweredon

and follow the prompts to download your free music.

We hope you enjoy it,

Sloan Churman

Powered On

Sarah and I were honored to be a part of a film contest. Luis Peña, Trace Sheehan, and Shawn Bennet simply created a beautiful short film and have been kind enough to share it with you. They are incredible men, and this section is to show them honor for their incredible efforts and art. Please follow the instructions below to see what they have created.

Photo Courtesy of Luis Peña

https://vimeo.com/43354278

password: sarah

Luis Peña, Director

Luis Peña is a designer/dp/director and the owner
and creative director of peñabrand, a San Francisco
design firm. After the earthquake in Haiti, he became
deeply involved with wehearyourvoice.org, a non-profit
organization working to help Haitians rebuild their lives.

Grace & Mercy, an endeavor of love, was his
first documentary feature, and Sarah's film is now in
competition at the Focus/Forward Film Festival. Luis
loves telling stories through film and photography and
is deeply honored that Sarah trusted him with her story.
~ elpena.com

Trace Sheehan, Producer

Trace Sheehan is currently the head of development for Preferred Content where he is involved with several upcoming projects including a Neil LaBute film entitled Geography of Hope, starring Ed Harris and Vera Farmiga, as well as a re-make of the classic HBO series, 1st & 10, which he is producing with Ice Cube's company, Cubevision, for Amazon Studios.

He is currently producing *The Bounceback*, an indie comedy set in Austin, directed by Bryan Poyser, starring Michael Stahl-David, Ashley Bell, Zach Cregger, Sara Paxton, and Addison Timlin.